WRECKS & RELICS

U-297

THE HISTORY AND DISCOVERY OF A LOST U-BOAT

The Kriegsmarine U-boat badge. This particular badge is an original wartime Schwerin - the best maker of U- boat badges. An award of this badge to a U-boat crewman was usually made after he had successfully completed two operational sorties or, alternatively, at the discretion of his Commanding Officer. Badge illustration shown here is to actual size. (By kind permission of Mr. Jamie Cross and thirdreichmedals.com)

RICHARD W. SKINNER

To find out about other titles produced by
Historic Military Press visit our website at www.historicmilitarypress.com.
Alternatively please write to us free of charge at
Customer Services, Historic Military Press,
Freepost SEA 11014, Pulborough, West Sussex, RH20 4BR,
or telephone our freephone number: 0800 071 7419.

HISTORIC MILITARY PRESS

U-297
THE HISTORY AND DISCOVERY OF A LOST U-BOAT

© Copyright Richard W. Skinner, 2002.
First published 2002 by Historic Military Press,
ISBN 1-901313-15-8

ACKNOWLEDGEMENTS

To Gail for her patience.

For providing material and information I am particularly grateful to the following individuals: Jak P. Mallmann Showell, Kevin Heath and Ian Trumpess. I am also extremely grateful to my friend Kevin Mathews for his support and enthusiasm which has made this book possible.

Fellow enthusiasts are more than welcome to contact me through my publishers at the address given below.

My publishers wish to express their thanks to Mr. Andrew Hendrie for his help in the project and for allowing reference to his excellent book 'Short Sunderland in World War II'; and Mr. Jamie Cross of thirdreichmedals.com for his help with the U-boat insignia. They are also grateful to the Keeper of Records and staff at the Public Record Office, for without their help and unrewarded assistance a number of important references might never have been uncovered.

Printed in the United Kingdom by
DC Data Systems, 95 Poulters Lane, Worthing, West Sussex, BN14 7SY
Telephone: 01903 525 695

HISTORIC MILITARY PRESS
Green Arbor, Rectory Road, Storrington, West Sussex, RH20 4EF. Telephone/Fax: 01903 741941

www.historicmilitarypress.com.

Since early December 1944 a wreck has lain on the seabed west of the Orkney Islands. This is no ordinary wreck because within its steel hull are the remains of its entire crew.

This was a crew of young men - the oldest only 29, and the youngest 19 years old. A total complement of fifty men lie entombed within, forgotten by most but perhaps remembered by a few. Here rests all that remains of one of history's most deadliest weapons...a German U-boat of World War Two, U-297.

These vessels were once the scourge of every ocean on the globe. From the Northern Arctic through the entire Atlantic, Mediterranean and even the Indian Oceans they prowled in search of prey. They were well named the "Sea Wolves" and all those who sailed the world's oceans were aware of their presence.

A few U-boats did manage to sink a considerable tonnage. There were the so-called "aces" such as Gunther Prien, the commander of U-47 who sank the Royal Navy battleship H.M.S. *Royal Oak* whilst it was at anchor in Scapa Flow, and Otto Kretschmer of U-99, who later became the "tonnage king". Along with their crews they were treated in their homeland as heroes and liberally showered with awards and decorations. For so many

Above: A photograph of the crew on a 11th Flotilla U-boat, U-312. The caption on this picture states that the photograph was taken in May 1944 whilst U-312 was in Norway. U-312 and her crew survived the war. (U-boat Archive).

others, however, such as the Commander and crew of U-297, service in the German U-boat arm would not bring such glory or reward.

By the time U-297 was fully operational and patrolling at sea those early days, or "happy times" as they were known, were long gone. Prien had gone to the bottom of the Atlantic in early 1941 and Kretschmer had been captured at sea and was now incarcerated as a Prisoner of War in Bowmanville Camp in Canada. In those early war years, the U-boat arm had been the hunters but now, in 1944, the tide had turned and Donitz`s "wolves" were the hunted.

The Atlantic convoys were now being protected for the entire voyage. On the surface fast and nimble naval escorts darted

Above: Another of the 11th Flotilla U-boats, U-959, pictured returning to base after a successful patrol. They are in fact nearing the massive and almost indestructible concrete U-bunker at Trondheim. Known as 'Dora One', there was a sister complex, 'Dora Two', nearby. The Allies blew this up after the end of the war. (U-boat Archive).

around, watched from overhead by aircraft from the newly constructed escort carriers that sailed with them. New and progressively more successful anti-submarine weapons systems were in the process of being introduced or improved. The end result was that more and more U-boats were being sunk, with decreasing losses suffered by the allied merchant and naval fleets.

This book is the story of just one of those submarines. It is a story of a U-boat on her first operational patrol that would suffer badly at the cruel hand of fate - a U-boat that was sunk as a result of the actions of another German submarine on a completely unconnected patrol. One that was sunk whilst using a new snorkel device that the Allied airmen who attacked her believed made such submarines almost undetectable. More importantly, this book is the story of the discovery of the wreck of U-297 in a location different to that hitherto believed by the relatives of the crew and many naval historians to be its last resting place. Only now can the full story be told.

THE AUTHOR

Richard W. Skinner lives in Portlethen, Aberdeenshire, with his partner and two children. Richard has never dived but has undertaken the research for many important wreck diving operations. His area of expertise is, in general, the naval history of the Second World War, but with a particular interest in U-boats. This, his first book, is the culmination of years of research that began after the experience of reading a classic U-boat book in 1978 whilst visiting the massive reinforced concrete U-bunkers at Brest, during his service in the Royal Navy!

U-297

It was at the Bremer Vulkan shipyard, in the German port of Bremen, that U-297 came into existence. Her keel was laid down on the 27th January 1943. She would eventually become one of 91 U-boats that were constructed with thicker steel and fitted with improved diesel engines and advanced snorkel equipment. These were known as the type VIIC/41 U-boats.

The snorkel was a device fitted to the hull of such submarines alongside the conning tower. Once the snorkel mast was raised and connected, air could be drawn into the boat by the running diesel engines. The exhaust gases were then forced out through a separate enclosed trunking system. Seawater was prevented from entering by use of a ball-float system built into the snorkel. As we shall see later, it was this interesting feature of U-297 that would ultimately lead to her loss.

After a construction period of nearly nine months, U-297 was launched in October of the same year and eventually commissioned into the Kriegsmarine on the 17th of November 1943. By this time, her Commander had been appointed.

The emblem of the 11th U-boat Flotilla which was based at Bergen, Norway, from May 1942 until May 1945. U-297 joined this flotilla as an operational patrol submarine on the 1st November 1944. It is not known with any certainty that U-297 had her own individual emblem. Some believe that a badge based around an archer was designed, but it is almost certain that U-297 was never seen with this painted on her conning tower.

Wolfgang Aldegarmann had been born in the town of Hamelin on the 24th June 1916. The early part of his naval career had little to do with the submarine service. Indeed, in April 1942, he became a Watch Officer in the 18th Minesweeper Flotilla. During November of that year he was promoted to First Watch Officer and transferred to the 28th Minesweeper Flotilla. Here he stayed until January 1943.

By this stage of the war, U-boat losses were mounting - both in terms of actual boats and the crews that operated them. As the war progressed, it became more common for men to be transferred into the submarine service from other branches of the Kriegsmarine without their volunteering. It is now known that Aldegarmann did volunteer, and in January 1943 he is recorded as having commenced his U-boat training.

This lasted until July of that year, when he progressed onto a U-boat Commander's training course. In this instance, he is known to have been on the 54th U-boat Commander's Torpedo Course. On 1st September he was promoted to Oberleutnant zur See.

A U-boat of the 11th Flotilla enters a reinforced concrete bunker in one of the Norwegian ports. Note the Iron Cross and Kriegsmarine badges on the officer's chest. (U-boat Archive).

Poland. This was a training unit, and it was here the crew would prove themselves to be seaworthy and fuse together as a fighting unit of the Kriegsmarine, ready to serve their purpose as a 'community bound by fate'.

In order that U-297's messages and mail arrived on the correct vessel she was designated the field-post number of M 54 472. As with all other naval fighting units, (M = Marine), this number would remain throughout her career. Incidentally, during the training period whilst serving with the 8th flotilla, U-297 was involved in a collision with a sister ship, U-298, in the Baltic Sea. This resulted in U-297 suffering a delay in becoming fully operational.

During her time at this training unit, U-297 first came to the attention of the British Intelligence Services. Decoded transmissions, sent by U-297 to the Headquarters of the 8th Flotilla provide a partial insight into the following months. For example:

4th December 1943: U-297 reported being anchored off the Warmuende Mole entrance as a result of thick fog.

18th December 1943: The U-boat informed headquarters that she was about to dive.

A few months passed as the training continued apace. On the 18th May 1944, U-297 left Pillau for Gotenhafen, (known as Gdynia before September 1939), from where she sailed three days later for vibration tests. Four days prior to D-Day, on the 2nd June 1944, she was instructed to undergo individual training,

In November 1943 Aldegarmann successfully completed his Commander's training. All that now remained was for a command to be allocated. Only a month previously U-297 had been launched and was in the process of being commissioned. All she needed was a Commander. So in November 1943, Oblt. Wolfgang Aldegarmann was given command of his first U-boat, the new U-297. With her Commander in place, U-297 was fully commissioned on the 17th November. On this date the vessel became part of the 8th Flotilla, based at Danzig - now named Gdansk, returning to the harbour at Gotenhafen on the 12th. As operational duties neared, U-297 gradually moved west along the Baltic reporting, on the 25th October 1944, that she had left Kiel bound for Sonderburg before returning to Kiel the next day.

Eventually her day of reckoning finally arrived, and on the 1st November 1944 she was posted to the 11th Flotilla.

This Flotilla, which was based at Bergen, Norway, from May 1942 till the end of the war in Europe, was not a training unit. Under the 11th Flotilla, U-297 was to become a fully operational patrol boat. On the 11th November 1943, she sailed from Kiel, and set out for the Norwegian port of Horten, south of Oslo. On this day she was not alone for another U-boat, U-877, reported having taken up position with escort vessels alongside U-297.

The journey was uneventful, and on the 18th November 1944 U-297 docked successfully at Horten.

Top right: The first of five photographs taken of Wolfgang Aldegarmann and his crew that have never previously been seen in public. This image of a young Aldegarmann was no doubt taken in the early years of his naval service. (By kind permission of the widow of Wolfgang Aldegarmann).

Bottom right: This picture of Aldegarmann, one of the five never previously published, was taken on board U-297 during training in the Baltic. Aldegarmann is wearing the thick grey leather jacket issued to U-boat crews. Note also the high powered binoculars hanging round his neck. (By kind permission of the widow of Wolfgang Aldegarmann).

Taken from the bow looking aft, this is an excellent view of the topside of a U-boat. Of note in this picture is the wooden decking along the top of the hull. As you will see later in the book this feature has been completely lost from the wreck of U-297. This picture shows U-959, also from the 11th Flotilla. U-959 was sunk by a Fleet Air Arm Swordfish operating from H.M.S. *Fencer* north east of Iceland on the 2nd May 1944. (U-boat Archive).

The first, and last, patrol

Above: An image of Wolfgang Aldegarmann taken later in the war. The author has since discovered that before the war he had been a merchant sailor and had sailed on the big passenger ship *Bremen* as the 3rd or 4th Officer. In this picture, we can see that Aldegarmann has been awarded the Iron Cross Second Class.(By kind permission of the widow of Wolfgang Aldegarmann).

Exactly a week after arriving in Norway U-297 sailed, on the 26th November 1944, with her crew of 49 young men under the command of the 28 year-old Oberleutnant Aldegarmann. They waved goodbye to their 'kameraden' on the dockside at Horten, Norway, and headed, as ordered, across the North Sea for British coastal waters. U-297 was instructed to patrol

area AN15 in the sea-lanes off Northern Scotland and the Northern Isles. More specifically she was to blockade Hoy Sound, the entrance to Scapa Flow. She was not alone on this patrol, (code named 'Diana'), - seven other snorkel equipped U-boats were on the same operation – U-1020; U-739; U-312; U-737; U-217, U-315 and U-278. The mission was to patrol near the Royal Naval base at Scapa Flow with the aim of discovering and sinking British aircraft carriers that had been operating off the Norwegian coast. The Germans believed, mistakenly, that they would be returning to Scapa.

U-297 was now on her first operational duty as a fighting unit of the 11th Flotilla, whose headquarters were in Bergen. The boat and her crew would never return to Norwegian waters. In fact they would never be heard from, or seen, ever again. The patrol appears to have been uneventful for Aldegarmann and his crew until events on the 6th December 1944 caught up with them. The sequence of events that ultimately led to the loss of U-297 can be traced back to the actions of yet another U-boat - the U-775. This submarine was on a patrol completely separate from that being undertaken by U-297.

At about 10am on that fateful morning the commander of U-775, on station east of Cape Wrath, spotted a number of destroyers belonging to the Royal Navy's 19th Escort

208

U 297

Der letzte Aal

Die letzte Kiste

Es
ist
vollbracht!

Obltnt. z. See

Obltnt. (Jng.) u.L.J.   Ltnt. z. See u. I. W.O.   Ltnt. z. See

Above: The Officers and senior crew of U-297, in this rediscovered photograph, standing on her deck just in front of the 20mm quadruple mount anti-aircraft gun. The date is the 17th November 1943, the day that U-297 was officially commissioned and her first Commander, Wolfgang Aldegarmann, appointed. Aldegarmann is standing in the centre. (By kind permission of the widow of Wolfgang Aldegarmann).

Group. Erich Tashchenmacher, Captain of U-775, selected one of these escort destroyers, H.M.S. *Bullen*, as his intended target. Just over a year old, H.M.S. *Bullen* had been launched in August 1943 at the Bethlehem-Hingham shipyard, Hingham, Massachusetts. Originally given the identity *DE 78*, she was one of the American Buckley Class escort destroyers. Supplied to the Royal Navy on the 23rd October 1943 under the lend-lease agreements, she was then renamed H.M.S. *Bullen*.

From a range of 700 yards, Tashchenmacher fired his T5 torpedoes. Moments later a resounding explosion could be heard - even in U-775. A torpedo had struck the target. The destroyer immediately began to break up, with the hull splitting in half. Another of the Escort Group, H.M.S. *Goodall*, closed in, dropping her Carley floats and lowering her whaler. The S.O. (Submarine Officer) on another destroyer, H.M.S. *Hesperus*, ordered that Operation Observant be immediately set in motion. This was basically a square search pattern that gets wider on each leg.

The asdic operator on board soon picked up a contact and *Hesperus* turned hard to starboard in an attempt to gain on the source. Sadly her wake capsized the whaler that had been lowered by *Goodall*, throwing those inside into icy cold water. In this accident both of the *Goodall* crewmen manning the whaler, as well as a number of survivors from *Bullen*, drowned.

A survivor from H.M.S. *Bullen*, Stoker Petty Officer Frank Hughes, later described what happened to his ship:

"It had just turned 10 o'clock and I was down below keeping the forenoon watch. I felt the explosion that lifted me right off my feet. I managed to pick myself up and felt to see if I

Left: The guest book entry of U-297. Such books were held by the training flotillas, and as a U-boat left for the last time, tradition demanded that one of the crew would devise and draw an entry for his U-boat. It was considered an informal 'thank you'. The entry for U-297 is entitled 'Es ist vollbracht!' (It is finished!). The image on the left is 'The last eel' and the image on the right 'The last crate'. No doubt these are references for the loading of stores and provisions prior to U-297 departing from the training unit on her first operation. In the centre is the signature of the Commander, Wolfgang Aldegarmann. Below his name, from left to right, are the signatures of Engineering Officer Oberleutnant Ernst Frieburg; First Watch Officer Oberleutnant Kurt Kraker; and the Second Officer of the Watch Leutnant Wolfgang Schneeberg. (U-boat Archive).

The Commander of U-315, an 11th Flotilla U-boat, is presented with a bouquet of flowers to mark the safe return from a patrol. This picture was taken either at the U-boat base at Bergen or Trondheim. (U-boat Archive).

was all right. I did not seem to have been hurt, though my ribs were painful.

"I looked round to see what was happening. All the lights had gone out. One of the stokers asked 'are you alright?' to which I replied that I was ok. I turned on the emergency lights and reached for my torch so that I could check the bilges. I noticed that there was a slight list on the ship, but for the moment we were dry and there seemed to be no water coming in.

"I then saw the Engineer Officer pass, (I could tell it was him from the uniform he had on), so I put my head through the hatchway and called out 'Sir, what's happening?' He said 'You had better come up - they are abandoning ship'. I got all the stokers up and out of it before shutting the hatches down. I looked outside on the upper deck and could see that she was in a very bad condition. She was sinking, and as I looked over the port side to the Forecastle, I saw she was awash.

"There were only a few left on the Forecastle by that time, and as I had no lifebelt at this moment, when I saw Mr. Crook, I asked him if there was a spare one. He said that he had one that might do. Stoker Dale said that his didn't fit him but, as it would fit me, he

The U-bunker at Trondheim - one of the ports used by the 11th Flotilla. This massive structure still exists, and since the war has been converted into small business units. (U-boat Archive).

would have the other.........I then went over the port side and started to swim for it.

"As I swam for it I thought I would have a rest and looked back. The mast was going over. Then, I saw the net and life raft and started to swim over to them. I again looked around for the ship. She was now in two. The bows were going up to meet the stern."

For many of the crew there was no doubt what had caused the loss of this ship. In the subsequent Board of Inquiry one of the ship's officers, Lieutenant William Daniel, simply stated that the torpedo "impacted the bulkhead between the engine room and the No.2 boiler room".

Despite such testimony, in its findings delivered on the 18th December 1944, the Board of Inquiry stated that it was 'not certain why the Bullen was sunk - there was evidence for torpedo or mine.' The report went on to note that no submarine contact had been made in good asdic conditions.

A torpedo if fired must therefore have been from a submarine in water that had already been swept. No periscope had been sighted or detected by radar. It did confirm that the

Right: Oblt. Wolfgang Aldegarmann and his officers on the bridge of U-297 during training exercises with the 8th Flotilla. Aldegarmann is on the far right. The officer in the peaked cap is Kurt Kraker, (see page 20). The small flag flying from flagpole on the right is the commissioning pennant. This was given when the U-boat was handed over by the builder's yard and became the property of the Kriegsmarine. On the far right is the extendable aerial mast. This is telescopic and would retract flush into the actual conning tower fairing. It was used for radio communication. Also of note, on the left of the picture, is the slightly raised attack periscope. Someone aboard must be looking through the periscope to starboard - the same direction in which Aldegarmann is watching! (By kind permission of the widow of Wolfgang Aldegarmann).

explosion had taken place on the starboard side in the area of No.98 section. This caused the after engine room and boiler room to fill with water - breaking the ship's back.

As the *Bullen* was being pulled apart by the flooding, H.M.S. *Goodall* did obtain an asdic contact on a possible enemy submarine. She joined the sporadic depth charging that was to continue for some 14 hours.

It was this activity, along with the final departure of the shattered *Bullen*, which was witnessed by the crew of a Short Sunderland that had been ordered to the site of the attack. It was the arrival of this flying boat that ultimately sealed the fate of U-297. By her actions in attacking the Escort Destroyer, U-775 had set in motion a sequence of events that would ultimately see her escaping undamaged, but a fellow U-boat, on a separate and completely unconnected mission, being sent to a watery grave with all hands.

Depth Charged

Above: A Short Sunderland flying boat similar to NS-Y of No.201 Squadron, flown by F/lt Hatton R.A.F.V.R. on the 6th December 1944. (By kind permission of Mr. Andrew Hendrie).

By this stage in the war, as was stated earlier, the Kriegsmarine U-boat arm was suffering terrible losses with both machines and men being sent to their deaths in ever-increasing numbers. Being a crewmember on a newer type of boat did make one feel a little safer, especially if the vessel had a snorkel that allowed longer periods submerged - away from the threat of aerial attack. However this would be U-297`s downfall, for on the 6th December 1944, whilst on patrol in the waters around Orkney, it was her snorkel that was detected and ultimately sealed her fate.

Some three hours before H.M.S. *Bullen* had

been struck, a R.A.F. Short Sunderland lifted off from its base at Castle Archdale on Loch Erne, County Fermanagh, Northern Ireland. As Flight Lieutenant 129070 Denis Ralph Hatton R.A.F.V.R. eased the mighty flying boat into the air he would have had little forewarning of what was to follow. The intelligence summary from Headquarters Coastal Command reported that 'apart from some activity off the northern coast of Scotland the situation is quiet'.

On a routine anti-submarine patrol, Hatton and his crew of eleven were flying a Mark III Sunderland, NS 'Y', of No.201 Squadron, 15

Group, Coastal Command - one of 12 of this type that the Squadron had available on this day. Airborne by 7.10am, Hatton turned north and headed for his allotted patrol area north of the Scottish mainland.

not known with any certainty that H.M.S. *Bullen* had been torpedoed by a German submarine. Such an order was merely a precaution on the part of the Coastal Command controllers. The subsequent events

SCHEMATIC VIEW SHOWING THE WRECK OF U-297 AS SHE LIES TODAY
Seen from her starboard side, and based on original sketches made by divers on site (see below).

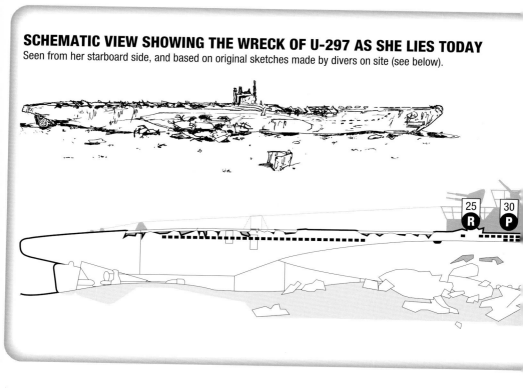

The start point for this patrol, position 58°30'N 06°15'W, was reached at 10.08am. 32 minutes later the wireless operator aboard the Sunderland received a coded message from Group instructing Hatton to proceed immediately to position 58°40'N 04°45'W. Once here he was to co-operate with Royal Navy escort vessels in the hunt for a suspected U-boat, though at this time it was

are best detailed by Hatton in his report contained within the No.201 Squadron Operations Record Book.

The Sunderland arrived in the vicinity of its new patrol area at 10.53am and at once the crew sighted the sinking H.M.S. *Bullen*, which, interestingly, Hatton and his crew believed had been torpedoed. After the last part of the vessel had disappeared beneath the murky waters of the Atlantic they circled over a number of survivors on rafts whilst continuing their searching. Nothing was seen all morning or afternoon, except that other on bearing 045 green. Hatton immediately altered course to investigate, dropping the altitude of the Sunderland from 400 to 200ft. At a range of one mile a considerable wake was clearly visible. In fact as Hatton flew up

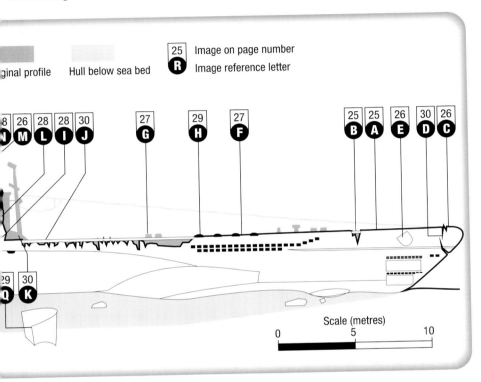

Scale (metres)

escort vessels (H.M.S. *Loch Insh* and H.M.S. *Goodall*) were now throwing out frequent patterns of depth charges while following U-775 North East.

At 4.43pm, just three minutes after sunset and in fading light, whilst the aircraft was at the approximate position 58°44'N 04°20'W, white smoke was sighted about 5 miles away the course of this wake, his navigator was able to measure its length - some 1,100ft! None of the crew could see what was causing the wake, (though they were able to calculate its speed as being between 10 and 12 knots in a North East direction), though we now assume that it was the snorkel of U-297. No doubt thinking that they were reasonably safe by using the new snorkel device, the crew of

U-297 were about to pay the ultimate price in proving that the theory behind such equipment was not infallible. Having reached the start of the wake, Hatton describes what happened next:

wake. The time was 4.52pm.'

'Three depth charges entered the actual wake, with the other three reaching ahead at spacings of 60ft. The wake and smoke

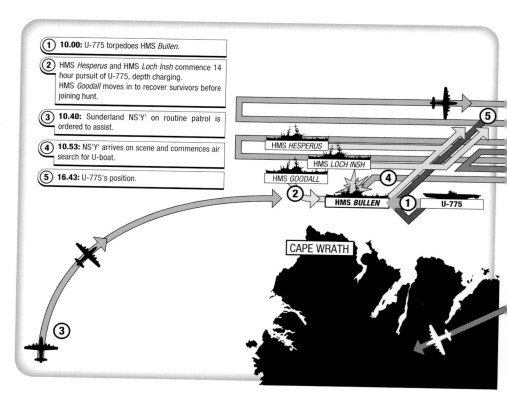

1. **10.00:** U-775 torpedoes HMS *Bullen*.

2. HMS *Hesperus* and HMS *Loch Insh* commence 14 hour pursuit of U-775, depth charging. HMS *Goodall* moves in to recover survivors before joining hunt.

3. **10.40:** Sunderland NS'Y' on routine patrol is ordered to assist.

4. **10.53:** NS'Y' arrives on scene and commences air search for U-boat.

5. **16.43:** U-775's position.

HMS *HESPERUS*

HMS *LOCH INSH*

HMS *GOODALL*

HMS *BULLEN*

U-775

CAPE WRATH

'Our aircraft crossed the wake's track ahead of the smoke, turned to port and made an attacking run at a height of 50 feet along the path of the wake from astern. Unfortunately, the depth charges failed to release, but as no faults were found a similar attack was made. We closed in on the same course and height; this time the depth charges functioned and a straddle of six fell in a straight line up the

immediately disappeared. Our aircraft circled the area and 5 minutes later a pear-shaped oil patch and ochre-coloured scum was noted. After a further 20 minutes this had spread to cover an area of 1mile by 1/2mile.'

This was U-297 in her death throes. The effects of the depth charges dropped by the Sunderland had indeed been catastrophic for all on board the U-boat. At least one of the six devices hit the U-297, or at least fell close enough to produce fatal damage. The conning tower was blasted beyond recognition. Seawater cascaded into the

advised them of the attack that they had just carried out, before returning back to the location. As Hatton continued to circle, his crew sent contact signals back to base. Finally, at 5.35pm, the Sunderland reached its

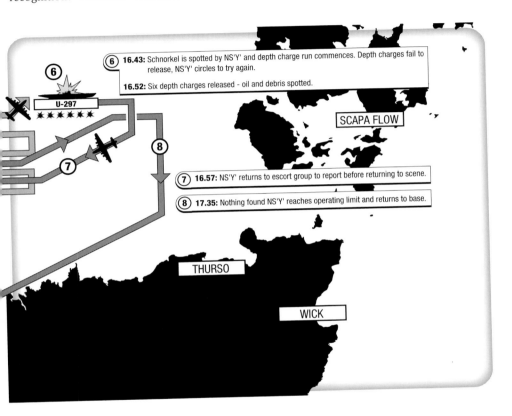

6 **16.43:** Schnorkel is spotted by NS'Y' and depth charge run commences. Depth charges fail to release, NS'Y' circles to try again.

16.52: Six depth charges released - oil and debris spotted.

6

U-297

SCAPA FLOW

8

7 **16.57:** NS'Y' returns to escort group to report before returning to scene.

7

8 **17.35:** Nothing found NS'Y' reaches operating limit and returns to base.

THURSO

WICK

pressure hull at an unstoppable rate. There was no time for any of the crew to do anything. Escape hatches or survival suits were pointless. As U-297 plummeted some 300ft to the seabed, her crew drowning inside, the Sunderland banked away. At 4.57pm, it reached the location of the nearest Royal Navy surface vessel and, communicating by R/T and Aldis Lamps,

P.L.E. (Prudent Limit of Endurance) and was forced to disengage the search and return to base. Hatton noted that at this point the first Royal Navy escort vessel was arriving at the scene of the attack. He later commented that *'the escort vessels could find no asdic contacts that night in the rough seas'*.

The Sunderland landed back at Castle

One of the crewmembers of U-297 who was lost in the sinking. It is in fact a picture of the First Watch Officer - Oberleutnant Kurt Kraker. He died aged just 22 years old. (U-boat Archive).

Archdale at 9.23pm having been airborne for 14 hours and 13 minutes. In his debriefing, Hatton reported that *it is probable this U-boat was destroyed* [as it turns out, a quite correct assumption], *though the photographs were failures owing to the failing light, and no radar contacts were made.'*

Despite his convictions, Hatton and his crew were never awarded a 'sinking' by his superiors.

Just three days before, on the 3rd December 1944, a top-secret report highlighted the fears of the Coastal Command headquarters staff in respect of U-boats fitted with snorkel devices: 'Very little success has been achieved recently in the detection of U-boats owing to the enemies adoption of the snorkel and their employment of maximum submerged tactics'.

Only the day before, on the 2nd, new instructions on the grading of U-boat sightings had been circulated to all Coastal Command Squadrons:

'The introduction of the snorkel and the extended use of GSR and radar by enemy U-boats has considerably reduced the chances of making a visual sighting of a U-boat and has increased the times when wakes, swirls, smoke etc may be seen which might be caused by U-boats. The following system of grading sightings and possible sightings is therefore introduced and will be brought into operation with effect from the 1st December 1944:

Grade A:
Sightings are confirmed visual sightings of a U-boat or some part of a U-boat visible above the surface, including snorkel or periscope.

Grade B:
Are visual sightings of a swirl, wake, or smoke which, in the opinion of the Captain of the aircraft, have been caused by a U-boat'.

So it was, paradoxically, that the fears of Coastal Command superiors about the perceived invincibility of the new snorkel devices being fitted to German submarines, (along with the lack of photographic or confirmed radar evidence), convinced them that Hatton had not sunk a U-boat. In fact the truth was that it was the very snorkel device fitted to U-297 that had directly led to its sinking - one of the earliest losses to a British aircraft of a snorkel fitted U-boat! Despite their success, not only were the crew of Sunderland 'Y' not awarded a 'sinking', but their actions were only classified as a Grade 'B' sighting!

The destruction of U-297 was so swift and so sudden that no emergency radio message could be sent. Indeed, no one in Norway or Germany knew what had become of her. Oberleutnant Aldegarmann and his crew had died a terrifying death in the icy cold waters. Along with hundreds of other U-boats and their crews, U-297 had become another "Iron Coffin" at the bottom of the sea, taking her commander and crew on their "eternal patrol". A whole year would pass before the German Navy informed relatives that their loved ones were 'missing, presumed killed in action'.

In the immediate post-war years it was assumed by both Britain and Germany that U-297 went to the bottom of the Pentland Firth after being depth charged by the escort ships H.M.S. *Loch Insh* and H.M.S. *Goodall* following the sinking of H.M.S. *Bullen*. It has now been established, with the privilege of post-war access to both German and British records, that H.M.S. *Bullen* had been torpedoed off Cape Wrath by a different U-boat - U-775. The Sunderland crew had witnessed the two ships, H.M.S. *Loch Insh* and H.M.S. *Goodall*, (who both subsequently reported having destroyed a submarine), laying out depth charge patterns on U-775. All

parties, including U-775, were unaware that not too many miles away was U-297, proceeding safely, so its crew thought, at snorkel depth on a course and mission completely unconnected with the events surrounding H.M.S. *Bullen*.

The last pieces of the story again show how luck was just not on U-297's side. Having sunk H.M.S. *Bullen*, U-775 survived the attentions of the two British escort vessels and, undamaged, finally returned safely to base. (U-775 in fact survived the war only to be sunk in Operation Deadlight). Finding nothing in the area of the sinking of H.M.S. *Bullen*, Hatton had widened his patrol area, eventually stumbling across U-297, who may well have been evading the events around her. Indeed, the other seven U-boats despatched alongside U-297 also seemed to suffer bad luck. Only U-278 seems to have had any success, whilst U-1020, another Type VII/41 submarine, was presumed lost in the Moray Firth.

As already mentioned, the end of U-297 was so quick that no communication could be made. Indeed, nothing was heard from the submarine or its crew ever again. As far as the German Naval High Command was concerned, everything appeared well with U-297. The situation was no doubt compounded by the fact that, as they had some suspicion that the Allies could monitor radio transmissions and obtain location fixes from messages sent from a U-boat, U-boat commanders were only permitted to receive and not transmit messages - unless under extenuating circumstances.

A Short Sunderland airborne. Unlike the aircraft flown by Hatton, this example carries camouflage paintwork.

Intercepted and decoded Enigma transmissions show that on the 14th December 1944, a message was sent to U-297 (and another) stating 'the admittance of a carrier returning from an operation is to be expected from tomorrow morning onwards. Keep a good look out and get right up to the entrances'. On the 26th, a further message to the whole patrol: 'Alteration to operational orders - you are free to attack all targets'. Four days later a long message with a specific line for U-297: 'Aldegarmann will steer for square Green PL 7650. Further instructions will follow'.

By New Years Eve 1944, the German Naval Command may have begun to realise that U-297 might have suffered a terrible fate. Over the following days a series of seemingly meaningless messages, sent specifically to U-297, were intercepted by the British codebreakers. It maybe that such messages were a coded method that would have been understood by Aldegarmann to make contact with base. The messages went unanswered. Finally on the 26th January 1945, nearly two months after U-297 was sunk came the blunt order 'Aldegarmann is to put into Trondheim'.

She never arrived, and from this moment on, as far as British records show, no further contact was attempted with U-297.

There is one final and, again, sad twist in this tale. Like the men of U-297, Flt.Lt. Hatton and his crew were not to see the end of the war. At 2.03am on the 14th March 1945 they took off in Sunderland NS 'A' - another No.201 Squadron flying boat. Just 27 minutes later the aircraft ploughed into the hills northwest of Killybegs, County Donegal. The Sunderland burst into flames and was completely destroyed, leaving no survivors.

Denis Hatton and his colleagues lie together in the Churchyard at Irvinestown, 12 miles north of Enniskillen in County Fermanagh.

The events described in this book are based on information contained within official documents in Germany and elsewhere, and which have been discovered during the course of three years research.

It is fair to say that the exact events surrounding the sinking of U-297 will never be known with full certainty, for all those directly involved in the event did not survive the end of the war.

Discovery

The crew of U-297 were seemingly destined to lie within their 'Iron Coffin' at peace for eternity in three hundred feet of icy sea, unknown and forgotten. Yet for some families in Germany, there is at last some closure, some sense of remembrance. Now, over fifty years after their deaths, two men from Orkney have discovered the final resting place of one previously 'lost' U-boat - U-297. With this discovery comes the need to change at least one entry in the history books.

Since the end of the war, both veterans associations in Germany, and the Ministry of Defence, assumed that U-297 had been lost in action elsewhere. Indeed, many of the relatives believed that the submarine had been sunk in the Pentland Firth. Now the story can be told, and surviving relatives in Germany can focus on the idea of a final resting place, even though they will never see their loved ones graves.

The two men who discovered the wreck, Kevin Heath and Ian Trumpess, both of Stromness, are keen divers. Kevin had been researching a wreck for a year or so, and despite advice to the contrary believed it to be a U-boat - but which one? On Thursday, the 4th March 2000, they headed to sea in the dive boat *Radiant Queen*, determined to answer this question once and for all. Commencing a basic grid search with sonar, they located what they believed was the site - an investigation of this seabed undulation was required.

It was Ian Trumpess who elected to enter the water and, having suited up, began his descent into the depths. *"It started getting very dark"*, states Ian, *"You know you are getting deep when you are touching 280 feet. I let my vision and eyes focus in. I looked over and immediately saw the wreck"*. Tales had passed from time to time that suggested that the wreck was that of a freighter. *"This was no freighter, it was a submarine"* says Ian. *"Although the 66-metre long vessel remains largely intact and in excellent condition it has been damaged in parts"*. Excellent research beforehand, good sonar and magnotometer searches and, no doubt, a bit of luck had helped Ian to dive within feet of the wreck of a long lost U-boat. For this team there would be no gruelling and uncertain searching. They had expected at least a 2 or 3-hour hunt on the seabed. Instead the discovery had taken the grand total of just 7 minutes! This tri-mix dive, made in fairly light and ambient conditions had taken Ian to a depth of about 86m (300ft). *"What I saw was the unmistakable shape of the bows of a class VII U-boat. It looked absolutely awesome. She was a magnificent sight"*.

Having located the wreck, it now remained for the divers to gain as much information from the U-boat as possible in the hope of making an identification. Starting at the bows, Ian started making his way along the starboard side of the hull, before rising up onto the

The *Radiant Queen*. This dive boat, operating from Stromness, was the base from which the exploration work on the wreck was undertaken. (By kind permission of Mr. Ian Trumpess).

The divers who have, during the course of three dives on the wreck, provided the images and information that helped uncover the facts behind the loss of U-297. In the foreground is Ian Trumpess, and standing behind is Kevin Heath. (By kind permission of Kevin Heath and Ian Trumpess).

deck. All four of the life-raft containers could be seen in situ on the deck forward of the conning tower - *"I noticed four hatch covers on the port side of the deck near the bow. This confirmed that this boat was a Type VIIC."* There are a number of different specifications for the class VII U-boats, but only the Type C had four of these life raft canister hatch covers. One container, however, actually lies open on the seabed with part of the orange five-man life raft protruding from it, showing the rubberised material from which it was made.

On swimming around, worse damage could clearly be seen. Where the conning tower fairing would have been is now a mass of protruding pipe-work and rusting sheet metal. The remains of the fairing itself lie on the seabed a few feet away on the starboard side. The extent of the damage around this part of the U-boat suggests that this was the area that bore the brunt of the depth charges dropped from the Sunderland. On the conning tower, where the bridge area used to be, one can peer through the open access hatch down into the conning compartment. On the floor of this section the inner access hatch into the actual U-boat itself can be seen. This hatch, which would allow entry into the control room of the submarine, is still shut tight. Beyond that hatch, just a few centimetres away, lie the remains of Aldegarmann and his crew. The open hatch that allows one to peer into the conning compartment, (where one of the officers would have sat and directed the U-boat via the attack periscope at the time of an attack), must have been blown open during the depth charge attack over fifty years ago.

It is here, amongst the worst damage, that the possible clues as to how this U-boat may have sunk were found. On reaching the conning tower area Ian discovered that this had been a snorkel-fitted U-boat. Such devices allowed a U-boat to run submerged for longer periods, reducing the need to, and risk of, running on the surface. *"I noticed that the snorkel was not lying in its recess on the port side afore the conning tower, but was in fact still raised with its securing clamp still holding it in place"*.

As further examination of the snorkel was being made, Ian made an even more dramatic discovery: *"The top end of the snorkel with its ball valve had been broken - no doubt as a result of the depth charging. The bottom end of the snorkel had also broken away from its swivel. On the left of the swivel you could also see the voice pipe laying on top of the air trunk - the pipe had snapped clean off"*.

Here then, the divers had found two places where, having been damaged by the depth charges, water could have poured into the U-boat. The crew would have stood little chance. It is probable that they had no time to shut the valves and that the end was swift. Kevin Heath believes that *"Initially there would have been absolute panic and horror in there. They were obviously given no alarm as they would have attempted to crash dive, but they took no action"*.

The wreck of U-297 lies, with a thirty degree list, on the sandy ocean floor on her starboard. As well as the main hull, there is much wreckage scattered across the surrounding area. During the early stages of the dive, Ian

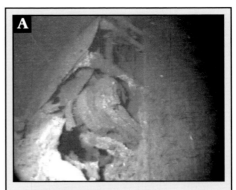

Shown here is the bow of the U-boat facing aft. At the centre of the picture you can see the windlass mechanism that was used to hoist in the anchor. The anchor is actually situated on the starboard side. The windlass would normally be concealed within the upper deck casing, but as it has been exposed, due to either corrosion of the casing itself or damage sustained during the attack, we are given a much clearer view.

Directly below the windlass is the portside bow hydroplane that was used to control the stability of the vessel - particularly when diving and surfacing. To the front of the hydroplane blade can be seen the curved hydroplane guard that prevented any fouling of the assembly by the likes of nets, wires or cables.

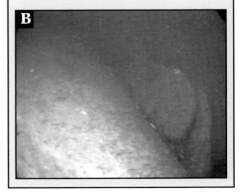

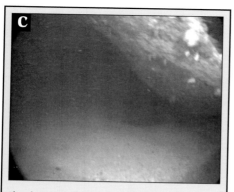

This photograph shows the extremity of the bow section - known to many seafarers as " the sharp end". At this moment, the camera is looking aft to the back of the wreck and moving from portside to starboard side. Whilst we can see little apart from the barnacle encrusted and rusting metal of the hull, what this picture does show is the starboard list of thirty degrees that the U-boat adopted when she came to rest on the seabed.

What is not evident in this picture is the fact that the bow of U-297 has been bent, and was found by the exploration team pointing at a right angle to port.

The anchor housing of U-297 with, firmly secured within, the actual anchor still in place - although covered in over fifty years of marine growth.

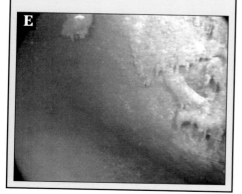

had already come across a part of this. Spread around the starboard side of the hull was all that was left of the 'winter-garden'. The 'winter-garden' was the two-tier platform located at the rear of the conning tower on which would have been mounted the anti-aircraft guns. Her anti-aircraft armament also lies on the seafloor, on her starboard side of the conning tower. Indeed, as described by Ian,

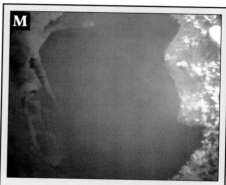

This picture was taken looking straight down through the open hatch where the bridge deck would have been. Peering into the conning tower a ladder can just be seen on the left. On the floor of the conning tower is another hatch, the inner hatch, which allows access to the heart of the submarine - the control room.

the matter of weapons would provide another clue as to the history of this particular U-boat. *"I could see that there had been no forward gun on this boat which showed her to be a boat lost after 1943 - all forward guns were removed at this time as the greatest threat came from aerial attack."* During his survey, Ian also visited the stern of the submarine in the hope that the U-boat's two propellers would still be present. If they were, they might provide a vital piece of information. It was common for a U-boat's number to be marked on it's own

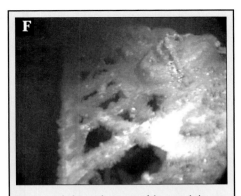

Here we are looking at the remains of the upper deck casing forward of the conning tower. On the right of the picture are the lids of the life raft canister hatch covers. During the exploration, Ian Trumpess was able to establish that U-297 had four of these. From this, the historian can deduce that the wreck is a Type C class VII U-boat.

Another shot of the deck surface at the front of U-297. If one looks at the period photograph of a U-boat on page 8 you will see that the deck is covered in wooden planking. This wooden planking rested on the metal criss-cross framework you can see here. The space underneath was partly intended to allow water to run off the U-boat's upper surfaces. On the wreck of U-297 this wooden decking has been lost along the whole of its length - probably as a result of the depth charge attack combined with the erosive effects of seawater at this depth.

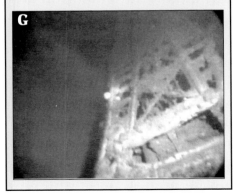

propellers. However, seasoned U-boat historians or wreck divers know that on its own such an identifying feature should be treated with caution. In the rushed, harassed and hectic world of the U-boat service of 1944 it would have been quite possible that one submarine may have been refitted with the spare or refurbished propeller from another. Approaching the starboard side, Ian found that the starboard prop was completely buried in the sand on the seabed. The port side was completely clear, but sadly devoid of any U-number. With his dive time marching on, Ian made his way down the port side of the wreck. Along the whole of the deck he could see that the wooden teak decking had long since gone - either as a direct result of the Sunderland's attack or the action of the water and currents at such depths. Halfway back to the conning tower, Ian came across a piece of equipment for which neither the author or dive team can provide an identity: *"I found a large frame work with wheels or pulleys - it looked like some sort of winch system"*. The team would welcome any suggestions from readers!

As his twenty-minute limit approached, Ian returned to the bow and his line back up to the surface. *"I saw that the port hydroplane was clear, but that on the starboard side was buried in the sand. I also noticed that the bow was damaged and pointing at right angles to port"*. It could be that this damage might have been the result of a steep nosedive following the air attack, brought on by the seawater pouring unchecked into the hull. Back on the surface, the dive team was able to collate the information gathered in the dive as well as the facts unearthed during research.

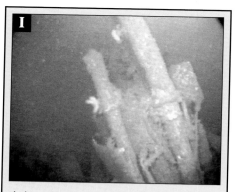

The battered remains of the conning tower. The fairing that gave this area of the U-boat its sleek appearance lies, separated from the wreck, on the seafloor on the starboard side. This is a front view. Taken looking towards the stern it shows the vertical pipe-work and other housings that hold both periscopes and the various detection gear apparatus. Indeed, on the left of the picture you can see the attack periscope, whilst on the right is the snorkel still held in place by its securing clamp.

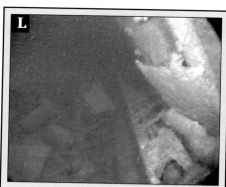

A shot looking directly aft down the starboard side. To the right can be seen the conning tower and at its base the engine exhaust trunking along with the remains of the starboard casing. On the far left and to starboard, just through the gloom, can be seen the devastation caused by the depth charges on the deck superstructure and gun platforms. In this area the 'winter-garden' once stood, parts of which are probably amongst this debris. The larger fragments of this platform lie shattered on the seabed next to the hull on the starboard side.

Another photograph looking aft from roughly the area where the bridge deck would have been situated. This allows a good examination of the framework upon which the wooden decking once rested on other areas of the submarine.

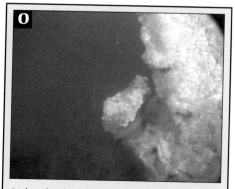

On the right side of this shot one can see a rusted pipe-like structure. This was the assembly that the attack periscope retracted into, and is a part of the conning tower. Note the remains of the sky periscope at the front of the conning tower.

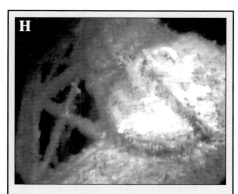

A close in image of the life raft canister lids that clearly shows the securing mechanism required at the depths and pressures at which U-297 operated.

Having examined the conning tower remains, Ian Trumpess made his way over the seabed to the conning tower shield that had become separated from the main wreckage of U-297.

They now knew the type and approximate age of the U-boat. They could surmise how it might have been sunk. This, its location and the evidence that it may have been operating at snorkel (and therefore periscope) depth appeared to fit with the attack report filed by the pilot of the No.201 Squadron Sunderland. Other U-boat possibilities as to the identity of this victim were also discounted by in depth examining of other anti-submarine attacks and operations. So how could they be certain that this was U-297 - especially when for so many years many others had thought that this U-boat had been sunk elsewhere? The final piece of evidence was provided by the video footage taken underwater by Ian Trumpess: *"Using the footage we were able to count the configuration of scuppers below the conning tower. These scuppers are like a fingerprint for a U-boat and each batch of U-boats has it own configuration. Comparing this information with the book 'German War Ships 1815-1945 by Gröner (Volume 2), Kevin was finally able to identify this wreck as U-297".*

Having, at long last, located and successfully identified the wreck site of the U-297, the dive team, Kevin Heath and Ian Trumpess, and the author would respectfully request that any diver visiting the site remember that it is an official war grave. Within this 'Iron Coffin' lie the remains of Wolfgang Aldegarmann and his crew. Their advice is look but don't touch - **take only pictures and leave only bubbles!**

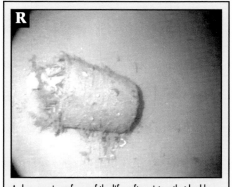

A close up view of one of the life-raft canisters that had been blown off U-297 during the attack. It came to rest a few feet from the main wreck, just below the conning tower.

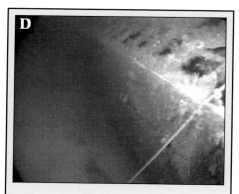

This area is almost directly above the anchor housing on the starboard side of the hull. Incidentally, the nylon rope that can be seen passing across the photograph from right to left is a guideline attached to a marker buoy on the surface. This allows divers to locate the wreck and help them on their ascent from the site at the end of the dive.

A view taken from aft of the conning tower looking forward. The cameraman is standing in the rough area where the 'winter-garden' mentioned previously would have been located. From here it was possible to see the remains of the conning tower fairing lying upside down on the seabed a few feet away on the starboard side of U-297`s wreck.

This picture allows us to see the of damage done to the area directly in front of and below the conning tower. The large diameter pipe running from the left of the photo to below the tower allowed the exhaust from U-297`s engines to leave the boat via the schnorkel . On the upper right of the picture can be seen the round inlet that the schnorkel was raised and then clamped to. This inlet fed air, drawn in through the schnorkel mast, into the boat whilst submerged.

A closer view of the hinged base of the schnorkel mast. This was normally hydraulically raised and lowered. During the depth charge attack the mast had been obliterated and fallen back onto the deck. This attack also destroyed the ball valve in the schnorkel that prevented water from entering. This broken assembly allowed tonnes of seawater to pour into the stricken submarine. It is believed that this was the cause of U-297`s loss and caused the loss of her crew within seconds.

In Memoriam

Commander
OL Wolfgang Aldegarmann, (24/04/16)

Engineer Officer
OL Ernst Friedberg, (03/05/18)

Watch Officer 1
OL Kurt Kraker, (17/10/22)

Watch Officer 2
Lt Wolfgang Schneeberg, (05/05/24)

The Crew

Josef Blaschko, (14/06/24)
Heinz Decker, (29/10/19)
Karl Geise, (05/10/24)
Lothar Guth, (21/10/24)
Walter Hagel, (19/02/21)
Willi Hill, (12/12/23)
Helmut Klein, (08/02/22)
Karl Kuster, (05/10/21)
Walter Loffler, (13/10/16)
Werner Muhle, (08/05/25)
Alfons Rebmann, (01/08/23)
Rudolf Rosch, (28/03/22)
Kurt Rosner, (25/11/22)
Kurt Schiek, (01/01/22)
Hans Steger, (19/09/25)

Otto Boas, (04/09/24)
Franz-F-Dilz, (01/12/24)
Theodor Glowacki, (24/10/23)
Oswald Haas, (09/07/23)
Alfred Hauptmann, (01/03/25)
Kurt Hoppner, (08/02/23)
Kurt Kolkau, (22/08/24)
Heinrich Langemeier, (02/03/20)
Herbert Maiwald, (28/05/24)
Wolfgang Musche, (06/11/24)
Josef Reisinger, (14/02/21)
Wilhelm Rokohl, (26/06/23)
Herbert Scharf, (13/11/21)
Hugo Schmiebusch, (17/07/24)
Wilhelm Steinhauser, (26/07/24)
Rudolf Wokoun, (26/05/21).

Paul Broscheit, (08/08/24);
Siegfried Ertl, (06/05/25);
Friedrich Granget, (03/12/15);
Heinrich Habel, (09/01/20);
Joachim Heppner, (15/08/24);
Herbert Kamper, (18/12/24);
Josef Krucken, (27/04/24);
Hermann Lochte, (16/01/25);
Karl Manz, (01/12/24);
Willi Niemann, (28/05/22);
Erich Rolleke, (11/08/20);
Werner Rose, (21/01/17);
Karl Shellin, (19/10/22);
Helmut Schneider, (22/08/21);
Peter Voge, (23/12/23);

There are no roses on a sailor's grave
No lilies on an ocean wave
The only tribute is the seagull's sweeps
And the teardrops that a sweetheart weeps.

(German Song)

The wreck photographs reproduced in this book were taken from the actual video footage of the wreck site. The cameraman was Ian Trumpess, who along with Kevin Heath discovered the wreck of U-297. I consider myself to be very fortunate indeed to know such men and to be trusted with such personal information given to me by them. Diving technology is now opening up places that were once unreachable to many, so it will only be a matter of time until someone else visits the area and sees the wreck.

The U-boat is now registered as an official war grave, which means no one is allowed to enter the wreck or remove any artefacts from it or the surrounding area. Hopefully, if there are any visitors in the future they will respect the wreck site for what it is - an iron coffin containing the remains of fifty young men cut down in their prime, like so many other sailors, merchantmen or submariners of so many nationalities. Remember, if you must visit the wreck site: 'take only pictures, and leave only bubbles'.

NOTES ON SOURCES

For those wishing to reference some of the official records consulted by the author and the production staff, the following would be a sound basis:

AIR 27/1174 (Operations record book for No.201 Squadron, January 1944 till June 1945)

ADM 237 (Convoy records, Operations Division, Naval Staff)

ADM 199/1693 (Anti submarine operations, tactical memorandum and operational orders, 1941-1945)

ADM 199/1694 (Convoys and convoy protection - anti-submarine operations, 1941-1945)

HW 18/380 (extracts from reports containing information about the activity of various U-boats, including U-297)

AIR 24/42 (Order of Battle, Coastal Command, 6th December 1944)

and ADM 1/18039 (Board of Inquiry into the loss of H.M.S. Bullen).